IT'S TIME TO LEARN ABOUT BADGERS

It's Time to Learn about Badgers

Walter the Educator

Silent King Books
A WhichHead Entertainment Imprint

Copyright © 2025 by Walter the Educator

All rights reserved. No part of this book may be reproduced in any manner whatsoever without written per- mission except in the case of brief quotations embodied in critical articles and reviews.

First Printing, 2024

Disclaimer

This book is a literary work; the story is not about specific persons, locations, situations, and/or circumstances unless mentioned in a historical context. Any resemblance to real persons, locations, situations, and/or circumstances is coincidental. This book is for entertainment and informational purposes only. The author and publisher offer this information without warranties expressed or implied. No matter the grounds, neither the author nor the publisher will be accountable for any losses, injuries, or other damages caused by the reader's use of this book. The use of this book acknowledges an understanding and acceptance of this disclaimer.

It's Time to Learn about Badgers is a collectible early learning book by Walter the Educator suitable for all ages belonging to Walter the Educator's Time to Eat Book Series. Collect more books at WaltertheEducator.com

USE THE EXTRA SPACE TO TAKE NOTES AND DOCUMENT YOUR MEMORIES

BADGERS

The American Badger, low and wide,

It's Time to Learn about
Badgers

With short strong legs and stripes on the side.

A digger fast, so bold and free,

It lives in grasslands, wild as can be!

Its fur is thick, a mix of gray,

To keep it warm at night and day.

With claws so sharp and nose so keen,

It digs and digs, so quick, so clean!

It makes a home beneath the ground,

A burrow safe, so snug and round.

With tunnels deep, it hides away,

And sleeps inside throughout the day.

At night it wakes and starts to roam,

To hunt for food away from home.

It sniffs and digs, it stops and waits,

For mice and snakes, or bugs and grates!

It's Time to Learn about
Badgers

It loves to feast on things so small,

Like rabbits, birds, and beetles tall.

Its teeth are sharp, its jaws are strong,

It chomps and chews all night long!

The coyote, sleek and quick as air,

Might team up with badgers there.

Together hunting, what a pair!

They find more food when both are there!

The badger's face is fierce and bold,

Its stripe stands out, both new and old.

But though it growls and shows its might,

It won't attack unless a fight!

It moves so low, it runs so fast,

Through grass and fields, it dashes past.

With claws like shovels, paws so strong,

It's Time to Learn about
Badgers

It tunnels deep where it belongs.

In winter cold, it stays inside,

It sleeps a lot, all warm and tight.

But when the sun returns in spring,

It wakes to dig and sniff and sing!

The badger's wild, the badger's free,

A clever critter, just wait and see!

So if you spot its striped-up face,

It's Time to Learn about
Badgers

Remember, this is its own space!

ABOUT THE CREATOR

Walter the Educator is one of the pseudonyms for Walter Anderson. Formally educated in Chemistry, Business, and Education, he is an educator, an author, a diverse entrepreneur, and he is the son of a disabled war veteran. "Walter the Educator" shares his time between educating and creating. He holds interests and owns several creative projects that entertain, enlighten, enhance, and educate, hoping to inspire and motivate you. Follow, find new works, and stay up to date with Walter the Educator™

at WaltertheEducator.com

www.ingramcontent.com/pod-product-compliance
Lightning Source LLC
LaVergne TN
LVHW052017060526
838201LV00059B/4071